D1717113

A BEACON BIOGRAPHY

MISTY COPELAND

Kayleen Reusser

PURPLE TOAD
PUBLISHING

Printing   1   2   3   4   5   6   7   8   9

A Beacon Biography

Angelina Jolie	John Boyega
Anthony Davis	Kevin Durant
Big Time Rush	Lorde
Cam Newton	Malala
Carly Rae Jepsen	Maria von Trapp
Carson Wentz	Markus "Notch" Persson, Creator of Minecraft
Daisy Ridley	Misty Copeland
Drake	Mo'ne Davis
Ed Sheeran	Muhammad Ali
Elon Musk	Neil deGrasse Tyson
Ellen DeGeneres	Peyton Manning
Ezekiel Elliott	Robert Griffin III (RG3)
Harry Styles of One Direction	Tom Holland
Jennifer Lawrence	Zendaya

Publisher's Cataloging-in-Publication Data

Reusser, Kayleen.
Misty Copeland / written by Kayleen Reusser.
p. cm.
Includes bibliographic references, glossary, and index.
ISBN 9781624693342
1. Copeland, Misty — Juvenile literature. 2. Ballet dancers — United States — Biography — Juvenile literature. 3. African American dancers — Biography--Juvenile literature. I. Series: Beacon biography.
GV1785 2017
792.8092
Library of Congress Control Number: 2017940570

eBook ISBN: 9781624693014

ABOUT THE AUTHOR: Kayleen Reusser has written 15 children's books and hundreds of magazine and newspaper articles. She has interviewed more than 160 World War II vets and published a book, *World War II Legacies: Stories of Northeast Indiana Veterans.* To find out more, visit www.KayleenReusser.com.

PUBLISHER'S NOTE: This story has not been authorized or endorsed by Misty Copeland.

CONTENTS

Misty grew to love ballet. Soon she was taking daily classes at Bradley's private dance school across the city. Bradley placed her in an advanced class with students who had been training for years. Misty had a lot of catching up to do. After school, she would ride a bus to the dance studio and stayed for hours. At eight p.m., she would ride the bus home.

Cynthia Bradley

In school Misty often knew the right answers to questions, but she was afraid to speak in class. With ballet she had a voice. She expressed herself by running, twirling, and jumping across stage. Ballet gave her life structure.[6]

As much as she loved ballet, Misty felt out of place among the other ballerinas because of the color of her skin. "When it came to being black, a lot of things were kept from me," she later said. "But I felt nothing would hold me back. I just worked hard and figured people would see beyond the color of my skin and recognize my talent."[7]

Within a year, Misty was performing her first show as a ballerina at the Palos Verdes Art Center. She experienced no stage fright in front of the crowd of 200 people. "I had performed a ballet solo in front of a crowd for the first time and by then I was in love," she said. "Each day I couldn't wait for the school bell to ring . . . so I could rush out . . . and head to the studio."[8]

Then, one evening, everything threatened to a come to a halt. When Misty came home after practice, her mother said, "Your lessons have to end." Her mother was concerned that between ballet and school, Misty had little time off. "You need . . . to spend time with your brothers and sisters," her mother told her. "You'll only be a kid once."[9]

If she quit ballet, Misty knew her dreams of becoming a ballerina would never come true. But she couldn't refuse her mother. What should she do?

Misty and her siblings (left) attended Dana Middle School (below) while living with their mother in San Pedro, California.

Sylvia DelaCerna with Misty

Now, watching the young dancers, Misty thought ballet looked different from anything she had ever seen. It seemed exciting, but she knew she could never be like the other dancers.

Her mother, Sylvia DelaCerna, was a single mom who struggled to provide food for Misty and her five brothers and sisters. At times they had lived with her mother's boyfriends or husbands or in crowded motel rooms. There was no money in the budget for ballet shoes.

Misty was also afraid of failing. *People will laugh at me because I'm no good at ballet*, she thought.[2]

Perhaps the biggest difference (in Misty's mind) was how she looked. She was only five feet tall and had brown skin. Her father was African American and her mother was Italian and African American. The other dancers were all white.[3]

Misty took a deep breath. Everything inside her told her to stay in her seat, but she had to try.

Pulling up her socks, Misty joined the class. Choosing a spot at the barre, she pushed back her shoulders and listened to the teacher. She didn't understand the classical music played during the lessons, how to count it, or how to find the rhythm. She had no idea if she was doing anything right, but something about ballet drew her in. After that first step, she continued to attend the weekly class.

With the help of Cynthia Bradley, teacher of the ballet class, Misty quickly learned how to perform arabesques, pirouettes, and grand jetés. In those moments, she felt on top of the world.[4]

Eight weeks after walking into the school, Misty stood en pointe (tiptoe) for the first time. For most dancers, it takes years to learn this skill.[5]

For much of her life, Misty Copeland dreamed of dancing as a prima ballerina.

Thirteen-year-old Misty Copeland stared around the room in awe. The walls were covered in mirrors. A waist-high wooden rail, called a barre, lined each side. Lithe dancers, in leotards and soft-soled shoes, stood tall. The dancers lightly touched the barre with their hands, while a red-haired teacher moved among them, instructing the students how to hold their bodies—shoulders back, chin up, toes out.

Misty squeezed her knees closer to her body. She had been going after school to the Boys & Girls Club in San Pedro, California, to watch the ballet class. As she sat in her gym shorts, T-shirt, and socks, she wondered why she was there.

Elizabeth Cantine, her cheerleading coach at Dana Middle School, had noticed Misty doing handstands and cheer moves during practice. "You could be a ballerina," she told Misty. "You need to attend a ballet class taught by my friend."[1]

Cantine explained that ballet is made up of graceful movements of quick steps, high jumps, and leaps. Sometimes dancers seem to float through the air.

An Unlikely Ballerina

Misty Danielle Copeland was born September 10, 1982, in Kansas City, Missouri. Her parents, Sylvia DelaCerna and Doug Copeland, already had three children: Doug Jr., Christopher, and Erica.

Misty's dancing talent may have come from her mother. DelaCerna had been a cheerleader for the Kansas City Chiefs professional football team.

Misty's early life was full of changes. It caused her to worry. "From the time I woke up every day until I came back home from school I was nervous about life," she said.[1]

Her parents separated when Misty was two years old. Her mother and the four children moved to southern California. Their father stayed in Missouri. Misty would not see him again for twenty years.

By the time Misty was thirteen years old, her mother had two more children: Lindsey and Cameron. DelaCerna married several times, but the family did not have a steady home. They often lived with their mother's friends or in motels. Money was scarce.

Misty never told anyone at Dana Middle School about her home life. By this time, her mother and siblings lived in two rooms at the Sunset Motel in Gardena, California. The children slept on the floor.

Romanian gymnast Nadia Comaneci won gold medals at the 1976 and 1980 Olympics. She was the first woman gymnast to score a perfect 10 at the Olympics.

To relax, Misty made up dances to Mariah Carey music videos. She also watched videos of gymnast Nadia Comaneci (koh-mah-NEE-chee) at the 1976 Olympics. As Misty practiced the same moves, she imagined great applause from audiences.

At ballet class, Misty's stress melted away. "I was grateful to hide from the chaos for a little while at the dance studio," she said.[2]

When Misty told her coach that her mother wanted her to stop lessons, Bradley was upset. She knew Misty had talent, and she understood that her mother did not have enough money for the girl's ballet lessons, clothes, food, and shoes. She drove Misty home after practice and talked to DelaCerna. Bradley offered to have Misty move into her home to continue lessons. She would pay for all of Misty's needs, including lessons and supplies.

DelaCerna agreed. That night, Misty packed a small bag of clothes and left with her coach. Misty was thrilled to be able to continue ballet.

At the Bradleys' home in San Pedro, California, Misty quickly fit in. She shared a nice bedroom with the Bradleys' three-year-old son, Wolf. Cindy's husband, Patrick, was an art teacher who liked to surf (they lived two blocks from the ocean). He agreed with his wife's decision to have Misty live with them, and everyone treated her like a member of the family.

With her mother's consent, Misty moved in with Cynthia Bradley, her dance coach. Bradley and her family lived in San Pedro, near Los Angeles.

For two years Misty studied ballet while living with the Bradleys. Their home provided a quiet place for homework, loving conversations, and encouragement.

When she was fourteen years old, Misty was invited to perform the lead role, Clare, in *The Chocolate Nutcracker* in Los Angeles. The production is a high-energy version of the classical ballet story *The Nutcracker*. Set in Harlem, New York, during the jazz era, the show features a diverse cast. It includes ballet, swing, tap, break dancing, and several other dance styles. When Misty played Clare in the show, Hollywood actress Angela Bassett played Clare's aunt.

The audience gave the cast a standing ovation. DelaCerna was there, too. She proudly clapped and cheered for her daughter.

Following that public ballet performance, many people called Misty Copeland a prodigy. In 1998, the fifteen-year-old entered the Los Angeles Music Center Spotlight Awards. This youth competition rewards local talents.

The Nutcracker, *written by Russian composer Tchaikovsky in the late 1800s, is the most popular ballet in the world.*

Misty worked hard toward her goal of being a prima ballerina while attending the San Fransisco Ballet School.

Misty won first prize in the ballet category. She used the award money to pay for a six-week summer workshop at the San Francisco Ballet School. The director of the school was Lola de Avila. She saw how hard Misty worked and offered her extra lessons.

Misty was so busy attending school, ballet practices, and competitions, she had little time to visit her family. DelaCerna began telling Misty that she missed her. When she told Misty she wanted her to move back home, the teen was crushed.

Again, Misty faced the real possibility that she would have to give up her dream of being a world-class ballerina.

Copeland met students from Lauridsen Ballet Centre during a visit. She had taken lessons there as a teen.

Family Challenges

Misty wanted to continue dancing and living with the Bradleys. She and a lawyer filed legal paperwork for her to become emancipated from her mother. Her mother did not want to let her go. The stress from fighting with her mother was too much for Misty. She dropped her request for emancipation and moved back to the hotel.

Misty transferred to San Pedro High School and studied hard, but she did not give up on her dream of being a ballerina. She began taking lessons from the Lauridsen Ballet Centre in Torrance, California, ten miles from her home. Her goal was to join the toughest ballet school in the nation, the American Ballet Theatre (ABT) in New York City.

In 2000, when Misty was sixteen years old, her hard work seemed to pay off. The artistic director of ABT invited her to take part in a summer intensive class.

By the end of the summer, school officials were convinced of Misty's talent. They asked her to join the American Ballet Theatre Company as part of their corps de ballet. The corps de ballet is a group of ballerinas who perform together. Their members make up the lowest rank of dancers in the company.

Misty was thrilled and accepted the offer. As soon as she completed her senior year of high school in California, she flew to New York.

She began her training with American Ballet Theatre by joining them on a trip through China. The group danced for two weeks in Shanghai, Taipei, and Singapore. Copeland performed as a girl in the waltz sequence of *La Bayadere.*

Finally, in 2001, Copeland officially joined the American Ballet Theatre. At just nineteen years old, she had accomplished her dream. She was a professional ballerina.

Copeland soon realized she was one of just a handful of dancers of color in the 80-member company. It made her feel lonely. She coped with the stress by eating Krispy Kreme donuts in her apartment after practice.[1]

Copeland knew this was not a healthy way to treat her body. She listened to advice from her mentors. One of them, African American Raven Wilkinson, had faced racial discrimination while touring with her ballet company throughout the South in the 1950s.[2] Another mentor was retired black ballerina Susan Fales-Hill. She encouraged Copeland to stay focused on her goal.[3]

With their words in mind, Copeland made changes to her diet. She stopped eating meat and foods with salt, sugar, and white flour.

Like most athletes, Copeland faced many challenges. One day during practice, pain exploded in her lower back. She waited a couple of weeks, hoping the pain would

Raven Wilkinson became the first African American woman to dance with a major ballet company.

The story of **The Nutcracker** *centers on a young girl's favorite Christmas toy, a nutcracker, which comes alive and defeats an evil Mouse King in battle. It then whisks the girl away to a magical kingdom populated by dolls.*

just go away. When she finally agreed to see a doctor, Copeland was devastated. She had broken a bone in her lower back. The injury could end her career.

Copeland kept the bad news about her back to herself. Kevin McKenzie, ABT's artistic director, asked Copeland to be Clara in *The Nutcracker*. She accepted the role. However, with her back pain, she had to give up the part.

After back surgery, Copeland knew she might never dance again. She wore a back brace for 23 hours each day for six months. Rehabilitation exercises took an additional six months.

Would she ever dance again?

Misty Copeland danced in the ballet Coppélia, which is the story of a doll that comes to life in the minds of her creator and villagers.

Meteoric
Rise

During her year away from ballet, Copeland continued to exercise. She swam and did Pilates. She had no idea if she would dance again, but she wanted to stay in shape. When she finally returned to the company, her body was strong and healthy.

She had faced so many obstacles that she grew discouraged. Some people said she should work with a less prestigious ballet company. Others thought she should join an all-black ballet company.[1]

Copeland refused to change. She still dreamed of being prima ballerina at American Ballet Theatre. Each day she worked a little harder to achieve her goal. "I thought brown ballerinas would benefit from seeing and hearing my story," she said.[2]

Her hard work paid off. In 2002 she was chosen to represent ABT at The Princess Grace Foundation Awards, one of the dance world's hardest competitions. There, she performed dances from the ballets *Tarantella* and *Don Quixote*. Although she did well at both, she did not win. "I was disappointed, but felt reassured that I had the loyalty of my company with me," she said.[3]

Copeland continued to focus on her dream. In 2007, when she was 24 years old, she reached the level of soloist. She was the first African-American woman to hold that prestigious position at ABT in 20 years.

The highest level was principal ballerina. If she made it, she wrote, "This could open doors for black women in ballet. It would all be worth it. That's what I'm doing this for. Not just for my own pleasure."[4]

Meanwhile, her dancing brought new fans to ballet. In 2009, American pop singer Prince cast Copeland in his "Crimson and Clover" video. After that, she danced in other Prince projects, including concerts and TV appearances.

In gratitude, Prince donated money to a struggling ballet company in New York. Copeland told a reporter, "They were about to lose their school and he's the reason the school is still standing."[5]

When Prince died in 2016, Misty was very sad. "I wouldn't be in this place in my career had I not met him," she told a reporter. "He pushed me as an artist in ways I hadn't been before. . . . He allowed me to be me on the stage, and explore."[6]

In fall 2011, Copeland reached another high point in her career. She was offered the starring role in Igor Stravinsky's ballet *The Firebird*. The story is about a magical red-and-gold bird that saves the life of a prince and helps destroy an evil monster.

Copeland so loved the story of the Firebird that in 2015 she wrote a children's book about it. In the book, she talks with a young black dancer. The girl admires Copeland as a ballerina, but she can't see herself in that position. Copeland uses the Firebird to show the girl that dreams can be reached with hard work.

Copeland was thrilled when Mattel made a Barbie® doll of her as the Firebird. "Having a Barbie® doll that is brown, and that is a ballerina, and that has muscles on her legs . . . [lets a child] envision she can be anything.... [It shows] it's okay to not look like the person next to you," she said in a video interview.[7]

While starring in *The Firebird*, Copeland felt pain in her lower left leg. She tried to ignore it, but the pain grew worse. When she went to the hospital, she learned she had six stress fractures in her tibia (shin). Three

Copeland's grace while playing the Firebird makes her seem as if she is actually flying.

were almost full breaks through the bone. "I was told by several doctors I would never dance again," she told *60 Minutes*.[8]

Copeland needed surgery for her leg to heal properly. Like the Firebird in the ballet, she worked hard to heal her body. Seven months after the operation, with a plate in her leg, she returned to the stage.

In 2014, in addition to the children's book, Copeland wrote a memoir called *Life in Motion: An Unlikely Ballerina*. The book became an instant New York Times bestseller.

More and more people began noticing the young woman whose athletic brown body and friendly smile were making ballet an exciting art form. In 2015, the editors of *TIME* magazine named Copeland one of the year's "100 Most Influential People," and featured her on the cover. It was the first time in 21 years a dancer had been on the cover of the news magazine.[10]

When Copeland danced *Swan Lake* with the John F. Kennedy Center for the Performing Arts, she danced with Brooklyn Mack. It was the first time two African Americans danced the lead roles for a major company.

Chapter 5

Never Give Up!

By 2015, Misty Copeland had returned to the spotlight after two career-stopping injuries. She had been appointed solo ballerina. She had traveled around the world, dancing in beautiful costumes while telling exciting stories. She had danced with pop singers and written a bestselling memoir. In August, Copeland danced in a Broadway play, *On the Town*, and in an ad for Dr Pepper.

She was in another TV ad in 2014. Called "I Will What I Want," it stars Copeland wearing Under Armour exercise gear while practicing ballet moves. In the background, a young girl's voice reads statements Copeland had heard as a child: "You have the wrong body for ballet." "At thirteen, you are too old to be a ballerina." As Copeland whirls across the stage, it is obvious she has overcome those criticisms. She has become an image of strength and determination. Just eight days after the launch of the campaign, the video had been viewed more than 4.2 million times on YouTube.[1]

Copeland continued to promote ballet and healthy living. Her health and fitness guide, *Ballerina Body: Dancing and Eating Your Way to a Leaner, Stronger, and More Graceful You*, was released in 2017.

Copeland is friends with Lauren Anderson (left). In 1990, Anderson became one of the first African American ballerinas to be named a principal for a major dance company.

In April 2015, she performed the lead role in *Swan Lake*, one of the most popular of all ballets. After that role, it finally happened. On June 30, 2015, Copeland was appointed prima ballerina for the American Ballet Theatre!

Her life changed quickly. Dozens of reporters interviewed her. A documentary about her life, called *A Ballerina's Tale*, was released. The next year a movie based on her memoirs was made. She appeared in a new TV drama about the lives of young dancers as they compete for places at a major ballet company. Disney created a live-action Nutcracker movie in which Copeland would star.

Perhaps the biggest personal event in her life happened on July 31, 2016. That day, she married long-time boyfriend and attorney Olu Evans in Laguna Beach, California. The two had met through Evans' cousin, actor Taye Diggs. When they have free time, Copeland and Evans like to travel, go to the beach, attend concerts, and cook.[2]

Even with all her success, Copeland has never forgotten her humble beginnings and the people who helped her grow as a ballerina. She continues to work hard, not just for her goals, but to help others in her community and around the world.

In 2015 the city of Los Angeles named an intersection after her near Copeland's first ballet school.

In 2016, Copeland met with President Barack Obama to discuss issues of race relations in America.

"I feel a responsibility to go as far as I can to break down barriers," she said. "It's hard for young black dancers to think they can make it when there's no one who has done it before. Having me there inspires them to stay focused on their path."[3]

In 2011 Copeland began teaching ballet at Boys & Girls Clubs of America. The next year she was recognized for her generosity by being inducted into the Boys & Girls Clubs of America Hall of Fame. In 2013 she helped organize the ABT's Project Plié to bring ballet to American students in need.

Copeland knew children around the world could also benefit from learning ballet. In 2015 she traveled to the African country of Rwanda with the arts group MindLeaps. She and program officials hoped to start a dance program there for girls.

Copeland spends a lot of time signing autographs and answering questions from young dancers. "One of the most important things you can do is surround yourselves with support," Copeland tells them. "It's hard to do [ballet] on your own. There are days when you are not strong enough to motivate yourself and those are the days when you need to have people in your life to push you, when you can't push yourself."[4]

Copeland is especially encouraging to girls who struggle with body image and whose build does not match that of a typical ballerina. "As a ballerina, you always stand in front of the mirror searching for flaws. You're so used to criticism from yourself and others that it's hard to remember that your body is something to enjoy, not just a never-ending fix-it project. . . . You can do anything you want, even if you are being told negative things. Stay strong and find motivation."[5]

Copeland remembered what it was like seeing a billboard of her on the Metropolitan Opera House for the premiere of *Firebird*. "I was in profile, wearing a red leotard, with my chest and back arched so you could see my full, feminine breasts and my round butt," she told a reporter for *Self* magazine. "It was everything that people don't expect in a ballerina. I stood completely still for five minutes, just crying. It was beauty. It was power. It was a woman. It was me."[6]

Although Misty Copeland stands just over five feet tall, she has created an image that towers in the world of ballet and in society. She knows it doesn't take a particular type of body to achieve one's dreams—it just takes a desire to dream big. As long as she dances, Misty Copeland will continue to inspire people to dream bigger than they ever thought possible.

1982   Misty Danielle Copeland is born September 10 in Kansas City, Missouri.

1984   Misty's mother leaves her father to move with Misty and three other children to Los Angeles, California.

1995   Misty attends her first ballet class at Boys & Girls Club, taught by Cynthia Bradley.

1996   She performs as Clare in *The Hot Chocolate Nutcracker* in Los Angeles.

1997   She moves in with ballet coach Cynthia Bradley and her family.

1998   She wins Music Center's Spotlight Award, Los Angeles Music Center. She is awarded a summer intensive course from the San Francisco Ballet School.

1999   After a bitter legal struggle, Copeland moves back in with her mother. She continues lessons at the Lauridsen Ballet Centre and completes summer intensive classes with American Ballet Theatre in New York City.

2000   Copeland graduates from San Pedro High School and moves to New York City to join American Ballet Theatre Studio Company.

2001   Copeland accepts an invitation to join ABT Corps de Ballet. She takes a year off to recover from back surgery.

2002   Copeland competes in The Princess Grace Foundation Scholarships.

2004   Copeland reunites with her father, Doug Copeland.

2007   Copeland is appointed soloist at American Ballet Theatre.

2008   Copeland appears at the Metropolitan Opera House in *Don Quixote* and *The Sleeping Beauty*. She is awarded Leonore Annenberg Fellowship in the Arts.

2009   Pop singer Prince invites her to dance at his concerts and in his music videos.

2011   Copeland helps create a public service message for Boys & Girls Clubs of America.

2012   She stars in *The Firebird*. She has surgery to correct fractures to her leg.

2013   Copeland returns to the stage to dance in *Don Quixote*. She is appointed Ambassador of Boys & Girls Clubs of America. She wins Young, Gifted & Black Award, Girls Rock! Award, makes commercials for Dr Pepper, and participates in ABT's Project Plié.

2014   Copeland performs lead role of Odette in *Swan Lake*. She appears in a TV ad for Under Armour. She publishes two books: an autobiography, *Life in Motion: An Unlikely Ballerina*, and *Firebird*, a picture book. She begins helping with a reality television series about young dancers.

2015   Copeland is named ABT principal dancer. She joins the President's Council on Fitness, Sports, and Nutrition. *TIME* magazine lists Copeland as one of its "100 Most Influential People." She travels to Rwanda with MindLeaps to start dance program for girls. A documentary is released about her life, called *A Ballerina's Tale*.

2016   Copeland marries Olu Evans. A movie based on her memoirs goes into production. Disney plans a live-action Nutcracker film and asks Copeland to star as lead ballerina.

2017   Her fitness book, *Ballerina Body: Dancing and Eating Your Way to a Leaner, Stronger, and More Graceful You*, is released.

CHAPTER NOTES

Chapter 1

1. Misty Copeland, *Life in Motion: An Unlikely Ballerina* (New York: Simon & Schuster, 2014), pp. 32–33.
2. Ibid., p. 35.
3. Ibid., p. 17.
4. Ibid, p. 37.
5. Nichelle Suzanne, "Pointe Readiness and What to Expect," *Dance Advantage*, April 6, 2010.
6. Copeland, p. 46.
7. Crystal McCrary, *Inspiration: Profiles of Black Women Changing Our World* (New York: Stewart, Tabori & Chang, 2012), p. 75.
8. Copeland, p. 63.
9. Ibid.

Chapter 2

1. *Misty Copeland, Life in Motion: An Unlikely Ballerina* (New York: Simon & Schuster, 2014), p. 18.
2. Ibid., p. 62.

Chapter 3

1. Misty Copeland, *Life in Motion: An Unlikely Ballerina* (New York: Simon & Schuster, 2014), p. 168.
2. Ibid., p. 160.
3. Crystal McCrary, *Inspiration: Profiles of Black Women Changing Our World* (New York: Stewart, Tabori & Chang, 2012), p. 76.

Chapter 4

1. Crystal McCrary, *Inspiration: Profiles of Black Women Changing Our World* (New York: Stewart, Tabori & Chang, 2012), p. 79.
2. Misty Copeland, *Life in Motion: An Unlikely Ballerina* (New York: Simon & Schuster, 2014), p. 267.
3. Ibid., p. 202.
4. Ibid., p. 210.
5. Yohana Desta, "Misty Copeland Reveals How Prince Secretly Saved a Harlem Ballet School," *Mashable*, May 2, 2016, accessed September 1, 2016.
6. Diane Pearl, "Misty Copeland Remembers Her Former Collaborator, Prince: 'He Will Forever Live On,' " *People*, May 2, 2016, accessed September 1, 2016.
7. "Misty Copeland Talks About the Significance of Her Barbie Doll," *The Root TV*, May 3, 2016.
8. Bill Whitaker, "Misty Copeland," *60 Minutes*, May 10, 2015.
9. Copeland, 255.
10. Michael Cooper, "Misty Copeland Makes the Cover of Time Magazine," *The New York Times*, April 16, 2015, accessed August 22, 2016.

Chapter 5

1. Niclas Hulting, "The Details That Make Up a Successful Digital Campaign," *Britton*, September 10, 2014.
2. Julie Mazziotta, "Ballerina Misty Copeland Marries Longtime Boyfriend Olu Evans," *People*, August 1, 2016.
3. Crystal McCrary, *Inspiration: Profiles of Black Women Changing Our World* (New York: Stewart, Tabori & Chang, 2012), p. 78.
4. Piper Castillo, "What's Misty Copeland Reading?" *Tampa Bay Times*, December 17, 2014.
5. "Ballet Star Misty Copeland on Injury and Success," *Sports Injury Clinic*, n.d.
6. Erin Bried, "Stretching Beauty: Ballerina Misty Copeland on Her Body Struggles," *Self*, March 18, 2014.

Books

Calkhoven, Laurie. *Women Who Changed the World*. New York: Scholastic, 2016.

Copeland, Misty, with Christopher Myers (illustrator). *Firebird: Ballerina Misty Copeland Shows a Young Girl How to Dance Like the Firebird*. New York: G.P. Putnam's Sons, 2014.

Gladstone, Valerie. *A Young Dancer: The Life of an Ailey Student*. New York: Henry Holt and Company, 2009.

Greaves, Margaret. *Ballet Stories*. London: Frances Lincoln Limited, 2014.

Mack, Lorrie. *Dance*. London: Dorling Kindersley, 2012.

Misty Copeland: Power and Grace. Photos by Richard Corman. New York: Ingram Publisher Services, Inc., Michael Friedman Group, 2015.

Regan, Lisa. *Ballet Dancer* (Stage School). New York: Windmill, 2013.

Royston, Angela. *Ballet (Love to Dance)*. Chicago: Raintree, 2013.

Royston, Angela. *Diary of a Ballerina*. Chicago: Heinemann Library, 2014.

Works Consulted

Bort, Ryan, Zach Schonfeld, Stav Ziv. "Katy Perry, Michael Jordan, Bill Gates and Others Share What They Wish They'd Known as a Teenager." *Newsweek*, May 27, 2016.

Copeland, Misty. *Life in Motion: An Unlikely Ballerina*. New York: Simon and Schuster, 2014.

Haithman, Diane, "Prince and Pointe Shoes: ABT Soloist Dishes about Video," *Culture Monster* (Los Angeles Times), May 2, 2009. http://latimesblogs.latimes.com/culturemonster/2009/05/princes-crimson-clover-video-features-abt-dancer.html

Hulting, Niclas. "The Details That Make Up a Successful Digital Campaign," *Britton*, September 10, 2014, accessed September 1, 2016, http://www.brittonmdg.com/the-britton-blog/under-armours-iwillwhatiwant-campaign-finds-its-audience/

Mazziotta, Julie. "Ballerina Misty Copeland Marries Longtime Boyfriend Olu Evans," *People*, August 1, 2016, accessed September 1, 2016, http://www.people.com/article/misty-married-olu-evans

McCrary, Crystal, and Nathan Hale Williams. "Misty Copeland." *Inspiration: Profiles of Black Women Who Are Changing Our World*. Stewart, Tabori & Chang, 2012.

MindLeaps International Artists Fund, https://mindleaps.org/iaf/.

Misty Copeland, www.MistyCopeland.com.

"Misty Copeland," American Ballet Theatre, http://www.abt.org/dancers/detail.asp?Dancer_ID=56 (accessed September 1, 2016).

"Misty Copeland—I Will What I Want," YouTube, Under Armour. July 30, 2014. https://www.youtube.com/watch?v=ZY0cdXr_1MA (accessed September 1, 2016).

"Misty Copeland on Broadening 'Beauty' and Being Black in Ballet." *Morning Edition*, National Public Radio, September 9, 2014, http://www.npr.org/blogs/codeswitch/2014/09/09/345297939/misty-copeland-on-broadening-beauty-and-being-black-in-ballet (accessed September 1, 2016).

Misty Copeland: Power and Grace. Photos by Richard Corman. New York: Ingram Publisher Services, Inc. Michael Friedman Group, 2015.

FURTHER READING

Stahl, Jennifer. "The Dance Magazine Awards 2014," *DanceMagazine.com*, December 9, 2014. http://dancemagazine.com/issues/December-2014/Dance-magazine-awards-2014 (accessed September 1, 2016).

Whitaker, Bill. "Misty Copeland," *60 Minutes*, May 10, 2015, accessed September 1, 2016, http://www.cbsnews.com/news/misty-copeland-unlikely-ballerina-60-minutes/

On the Internet

American Ballet Theatre
http://www.abt.org/

Misty Copeland Biography
http://www.biography.com/people/misty-copeland

Official Web Site of Misty Copeland
http://mistycopeland.com/

GLOSSARY

arabesque (ar-ah-BESK)—A type of step in which a dancer balances on one leg with other stretched out behind.

barre (BAR)—Wooden handrail that runs around ballet studios to help dancers balance when doing warm-up exercises.

company (KUM-puh-nee)—A group of people joined together for a common goal.

discrimination (dis-krih-mih-NAY-shun)—Setting a person apart based on the group that person belongs to, rather than on individual merit.

emancipate (ee-MAN-sih-payt)—To become free from another person's authority.

en (or on) pointe (POYNT)—The motion of dancing on tips of toes with help from stiffened shoes called pointe shoes. Usually only females dance on pointe.

interpretation (in-tur-preh-TAY-shun)—Artistic explanation of a performance.

leotard (LEE-uh-tard)—Snug one-piece stretchy garment covering the entire torso.

Pilates (pih-LAH-tees)—A group of exercises that improve physical strength, flexibility, and posture.

pirouette (pir-oo-ET)—A turning step, twirl, or spin.

plié (plee-AY)—A dance movement of bending of the knee or knees.

prestigious (pres-TIDJ-us)—Honored; esteemed.

principal (PRIN-suh-pul)—Main; highest.

prodigy (PRAH-dih-jee)—A person, especially a child, having extraordinary talent.

professional (pruh-FEH-shuh-nul)—A person who takes part in an activity for money rather than simply for fun.

rehabilitation (ree-hah-bil-ih-TAY-shun)—The process of regaining strength after an injury or illness.

INDEX